CONTENTS

Nathan Lane as Max Bialystock and Matthew Broderick as Leo Bloom
photo: Paul Kolnik

Cady Huffman as Ul
photo: Paul Koln

Gary Beach as Roger de Bris and Roger Bart as Carmen Ghia
photo: Paul Kolnik

Cady Huffman as Ulla and Matthew Broderick as Leo in "That Face"
photo: Paul Kolnik

Brad Oscar as Franz Liebkind singing "In Old Bavaria"
photo: Paul Kolnik

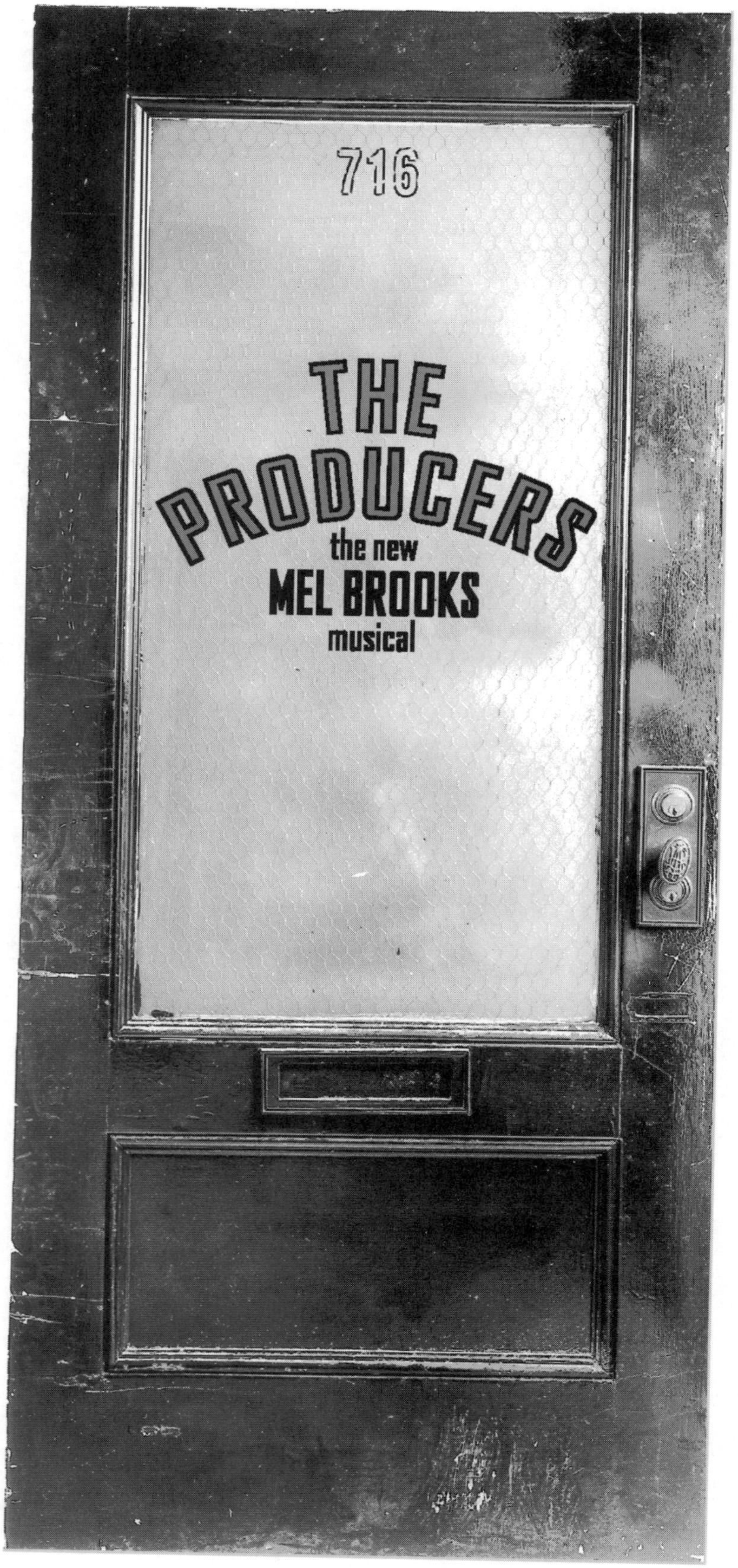
716
THE
PRODUCERS
the new
MEL BROOKS
musical

THE STORY

Spring in New York, 1959. Evening. The scene is Shubert Alley, outside the Shubert Theatre, Broadway's famed house of hits. But not tonight. Because the curtain has just come down on producer Max Bialystock's latest fiasco, a musical version of *Hamlet*, called *Funny Boy* ("Opening Night").

Later the same evening, Max, crushed but undaunted, stands in Shubert Alley surrounded by a ragtag chorus of after-midnight Broadway denizens. Angrily, he announces that he once was—and will be again—"The King of Broadway."

A few days later, a nerdy, timid accountant, Leo Bloom, shows up at Max's office to do his books. Leo casually notes that a producer could actually make more money with a flop than with a hit. "You could raise a million dollars, put on a hundred thousand dollar failure, and keep the rest for yourself." Max immediately seizes upon this idea and implores Leo to join him in this bold—albeit slightly illegal—scheme ("We Can Do It").

Back at his desk in the miserably Dickensian accounting firm where he earns fifty dollars a week, Leo drifts into a fantasy, in which he is a famed Broadway impresario surrounded by a bevy of gorgeous chorus girls ("I Wanna Be a Producer").

After quitting his job, Leo hurries off to join Max in his office. They go into business together as "Bialystock & Bloom, Theatrical Producers." The partners' first order of business: Find the worst play ever written. They find it. A disaster, a catastrophe, a guaranteed-to-close-in-one-night beauty: *Springtime for Hitler, A Gay Romp with Adolf and Eva at Berchtesgaden*, written by a nutsy neo-Nazi playwright and pigeon fancier named Franz Liebkind.

We now meet Liebkind on the rooftop of his Greenwich Village tenement, as he reminisces with his homing pigeons about the good old days "In Old Bavaria." When Max and Leo now turn up on the rooftop, Franz is overjoyed that they wish to produce his play on Broadway. He refuses to permit them to do so, however, until they agree to join him in singing and dancing Hitler's favorite tune, "Der Guten Tag Hop-Clop." Max and Leo hop, clop and ultimately depart with Franz's signature on a Broadway contract.

Next stop, the Upper East Side townhouse of Broadway's worst director, Roger de Bris, and his "common-law assistant" Carmen Ghia. Roger wants nothing to do with *Springtime*—"World War Two? Too dark, too depressing!" —and is joined by Carmen and his production team in proclaiming his credo: "Keep It Gay." Roger is finally persuaded by Max and Leo to direct *Springtime*.

Back in the office, triumphant, with the Broadway rights to the worst play ever written and a signed contract with the worst director who ever lived, Max and Leo are visited by a knockout of a Swedish blonde named Ulla. She wishes to audition for them, and audition she does, all over the office ("When You Got It, Flaunt It").

Next step, the money. Max sets out to raise two million dollars by launching himself into Little Old Lady Land. His description of how he does "it" ("Along Came Bialy") segues into a full-company Act One finale celebrating Bialystock & Bloom's forthcoming Broadway production of *Springtime for Hitler*, "a new neo-Nazi musical."

Act Two opens in Bialystock & Bloom's office, now totally redone by Ulla in Swedish-modern. When Ulla and Leo are left alone by Max, they reveal their mutual stirrings of love ("That Face").

Auditions. Who will play the coveted role of Adolf Hitler? Franz Liebkind sweeps away all other contenders with his razzmatazz Broadway rendition of the ever-popular "Haben Sie Gehört Das Deutsche Band?"

Once again outside the Shubert Theatre—this time it is "Opening Night (Reprise)" for *Springtime for Hitler*. Leo commits a huge theatrical gaffe when he innocently wishes everyone "good luck." Roger, Carmen and Franz, aghast, immediately explain to him that "You Never Say Good Luck on Opening Night." Meanwhile, Max, to ensure failure, is sneakily saying "good luck" to everyone in sight. As bad luck would have it, Franz breaks his leg, and Roger nervously agrees to go on as Hitler in his place.

Now onstage at the Shubert Theatre, Roger, as Hitler, leads the company in a spirited salute to the Third Reich ("Springtime for Hitler"). Disaster! It's a success! The critics love *Springtime*, calling it "a satirical masterpiece," "a surprise smash," and "the best musical of the decade." Stunned and bewildered, Max and Leo stagger back to their office where they recite their litany of woe: "Where Did We Go Right?" Max is arrested, and Leo scrams to Rio with Ulla and the two million dollars.

Alone in a jail cell awaiting trial, Max is crushed to get a postcard from Leo and Ulla cheerfully letting him know what a great time they are having without him. Tossing aside the card, Max vents his anger and dismay ("Betrayed").

A courtroom. Max has been found guilty and is about to be sentenced when Leo bursts in, back from Rio to turn himself in and take his place at Max's side. Why did he come back? Because in Rio—even though he had Ulla and two million dollars, everything he'd ever dreamed of—he realized what Max really meant to him ("'Til Him"). Max and Leo are together again, and will be for some time to come. They've been sentenced to five years in Sing Sing.

Sing Sing. Max and Leo put on their all-singing, all-dancing, all-convict production, *Prisoners of Love*. Good news! Having brought "joy and laughter into the hearts of every murderer, rapist and sex maniac in Sing Sing," the governor has granted them a full pardon! They're free! Next stop, Broadway!

The stage of the Shubert. The Broadway version of Bialystock & Bloom's *Prisoners of Love* is reprised in all its glitzy glory, starring Roger de Bris and a chorus of gorgeous, scantily-clad girl convicts.

Finally, the scene is once again Shubert Alley, where Leo and Max, on top of the world as Broadway's most successful producers, celebrate to the tune of "Prisoners of Love" ("Leo and Max"). Happy at last, they walk off into the sunset as the final curtain falls. At the end of the bows, Max and Leo lead the entire company in a final farewell ("Goodbye").

OPENING NIGHT

Music and Lyrics by
Mel Brooks

Fast 2 ♩ = 160

16

worst show ___ in town! _____ Oh, we

want - ed to stand up and hiss, _____ We've seen

shit but nev - er like this! _____

Max Bi - al -

THE KING OF BROADWAY

Music and Lyrics by
Mel Brooks

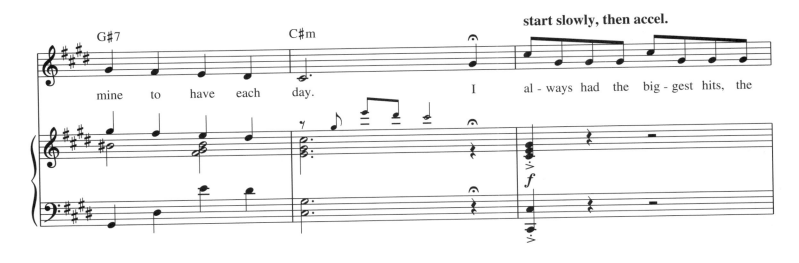

Fast 4 ♩ = 156

tux — that's two __ weeks o - ver due. __

CHORUS:

Poor Bi-al-ly, what a schmoo-zer, poor Bi-al-y, what a shame.

Rent-ed __ tux __ o - ver

Poor Bi-al-ly, what a lo-ser, poor Bi-al-ly, Good-bye fame!

due __ way o-ver due

28

WE CAN DO IT

Music and Lyrics by
Mel Brooks

MAX:

What did Lew-is say to Clark when ev-'ry-thing looked bleak?

What did Sir Ed-mund say to Ten-zing as they strug-gled t'ward Ev-er-est's peak?

What did Wash-ing-ton say to his troops be - fore they crossed the Del-a-ware? _

Moderately Slow 2

LEO: What did they say?

34

MAX: You miserable, cowardly, wretched little caterpillar.
Don't you ever want to become a butterfly?
Don't you want to spread your wings...

cresc. (dialogue continues)

...and flap your way to glory?

LEO:

MAX: Mis - ter Bi - al - y - stock, please
We can   do it,   we   can

I WANNA BE A PRODUCER

Music and Lyrics by
Mel Brooks

43

44

46

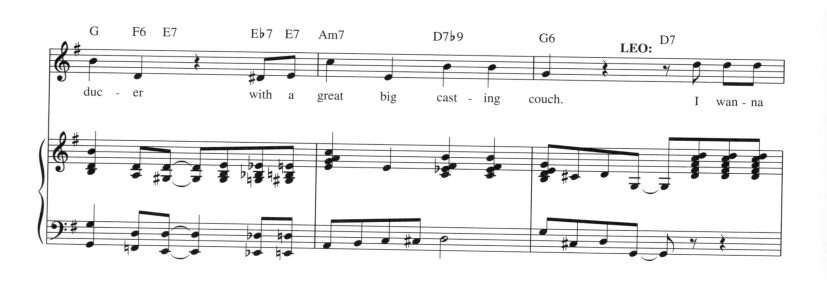

48

IN OLD BAVARIA

Music and Lyrics by
Mel Brooks

DER GUTEN TAG HOP-CLOP

Music and Lyrics by
Mel Brooks

KEEP IT GAY

Music and Lyrics by
Mel Brooks

Lightly, moderately slow

ROGER: The thea-ter's so ob-sessed with dra-mas so de-pressed, it's

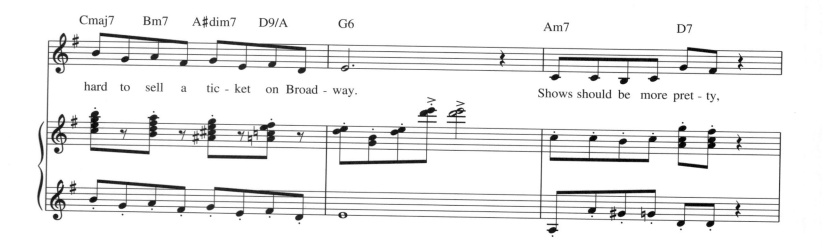

hard to sell a tic-ket on Broad-way. Shows should be more pret-ty,

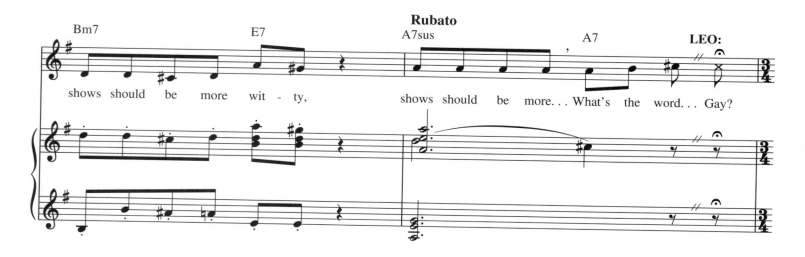

shows should be more wit-ty, shows should be more... What's the word... Gay?

59

WHEN YOU GOT IT, FLAUNT IT

Music and Lyrics by
Mel Brooks

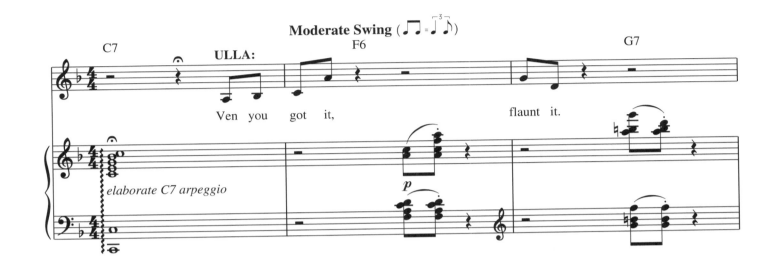

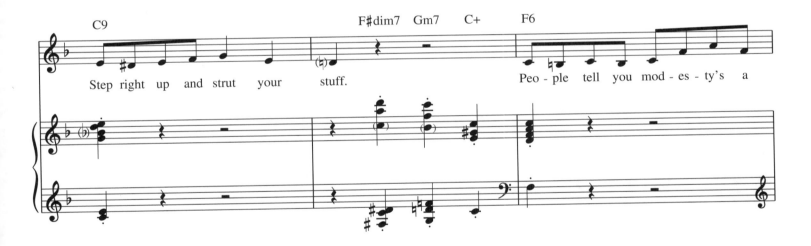

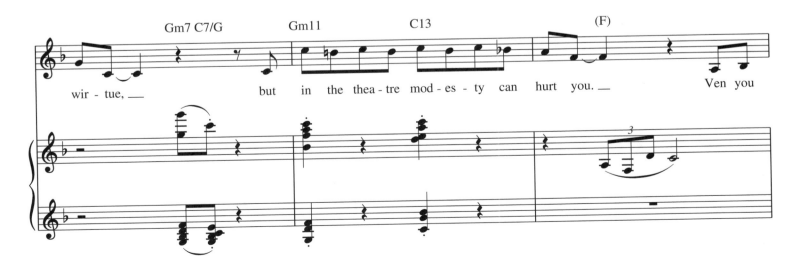

"Going home"

ALONG CAME BIALY

Music and Lyrics by
Mel Brooks

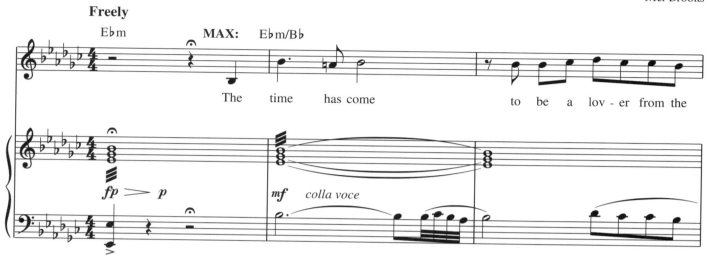

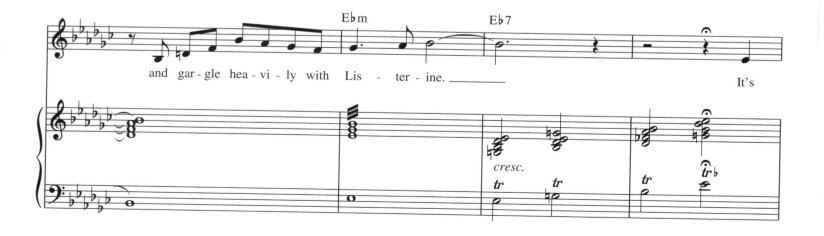

72

THAT FACE

Music and Lyrics by
Mel Brooks

HABEN SIE GEHÖRT DAS DEUTSCHE BAND?
(Have You Ever Heard the German Band?)

Music and Lyrics by
Mel Brooks

82

84

YOU NEVER SAY GOOD LUCK ON OPENING NIGHT

Music and Lyrics by
Mel Brooks

said, you are dead, you will get the worst re-views you've ev-er

MAX: Good luck!

ROGER: read. E-ven at the Com-é-die Fran-caise on the

op-'ning night they are scared. "Bon chance mes-a-mis" no one

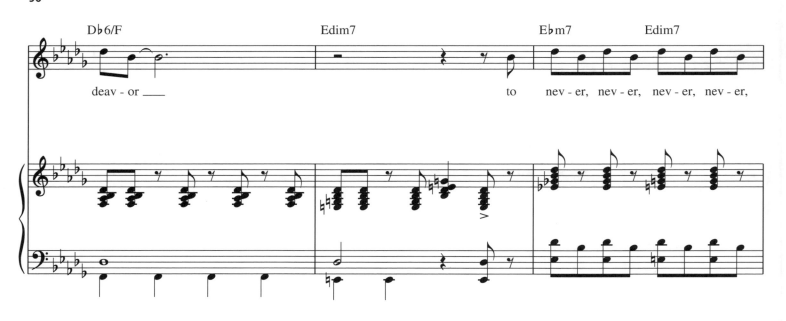

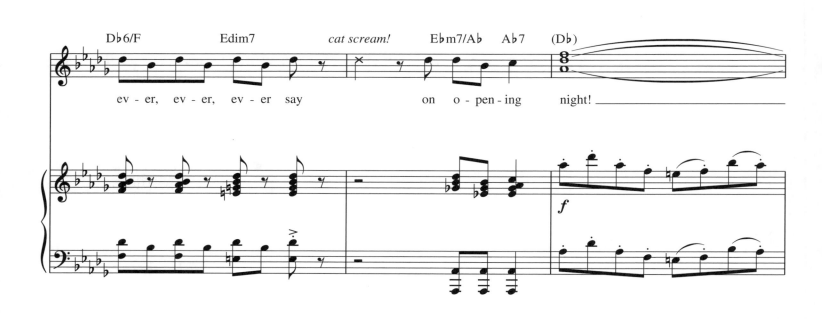

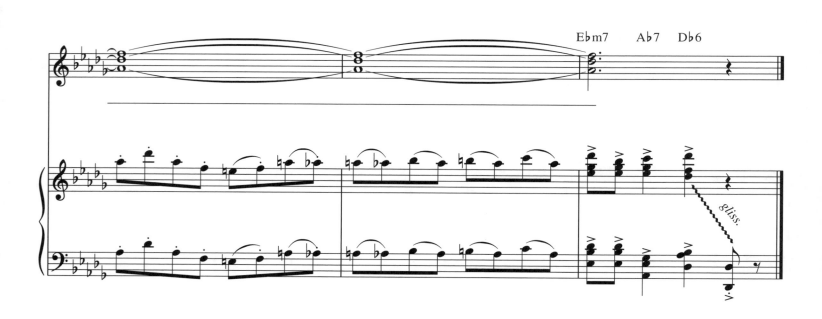

SPRINGTIME FOR HITLER

Music and Lyrics by
Mel Brooks

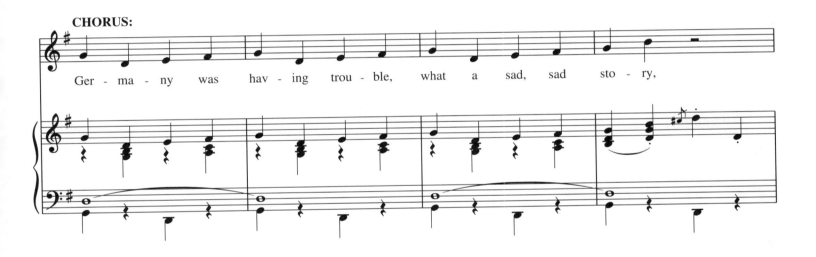

92

96

HEIL MYSELF

Music and Lyrics by
Mel Brooks

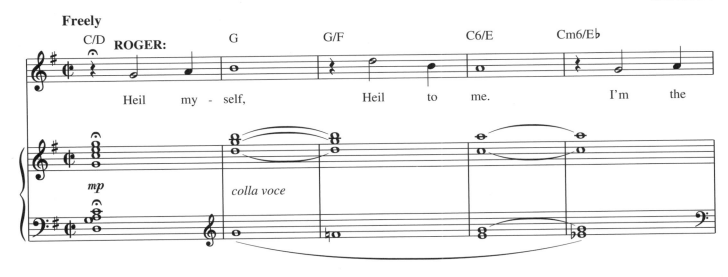

*Until noted, the downstemmed male notes sound as written (normally, these notes would appear an octave higher)

*Normal male voice notation

*traditional unison, males sing 8vb

*Male notes as written (normally would appear an octave higher)

WHERE DID WE GO RIGHT?

Music and Lyrics by
Mel Brooks

Moderately

MAX: *spoken*

The show was lou-sy and long, we did ev-'ry-thing wrong. Where did we go

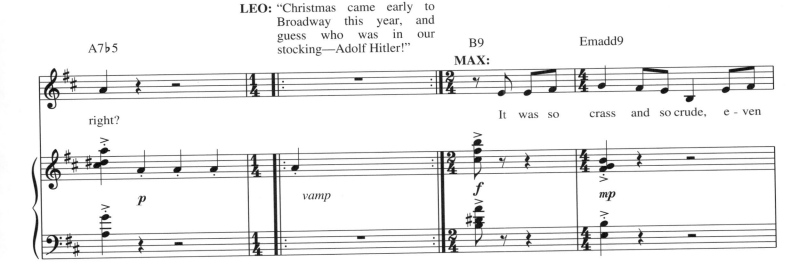

right?

LEO: "Christmas came early to Broadway this year, and guess who was in our stocking—Adolf Hitler!"

MAX:

It was so crass and so crude, e-ven

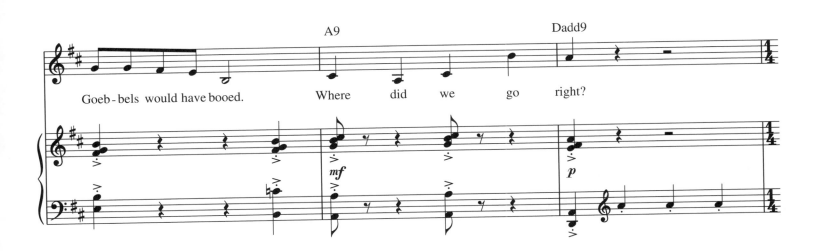

Goeb-bels would have booed. Where did we go right?

110

LEO: "Last night a star was born on Broadway—the lovely Miss Ulla Inga Hansen Benson Yonsen Tallen-Hallen Svan-Svanson. We predict that her name will soon be up in lights. If they can find enough bulbs."

112

BETRAYED

Music and Lyrics by
Mel Brooks

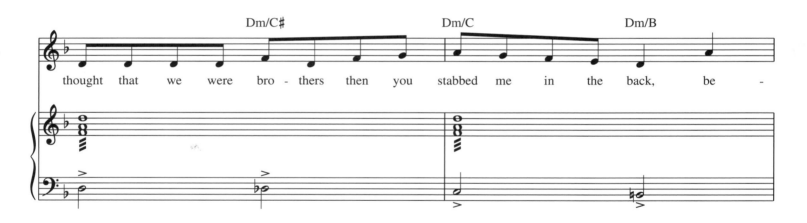

116

MAX: I'm drowning! I'm drowning here! I'm going down for the last time! I see my whole life flashing before my eyes!

(Spoken above the "bucolic" interlude)
MAX: I see a weathered old farmhouse, and a white picket fence. I'm running through fields of alfalfa with my collie, Rex.
And I see my mother, standing on the back porch, in a worn but clean gingham gown, and I hear her calling out to me,
"Alvin! Alvin! Don't forget your chores. The wood needs a cordin' and the cows need a milkin'. Alvin, Alvin..."

Bucolic, in 4

Wait a minute, my name's not
Alvin. That's not my life. I'm not
a hillbilly! I grew up in the Bronx!

Leo's taken everything, even my past.

'TIL HIM

Music and Lyrics by
Mel Brooks

128

PRISONERS OF LOVE
(Leo & Max)

Music and Lyrics by
Mel Brooks

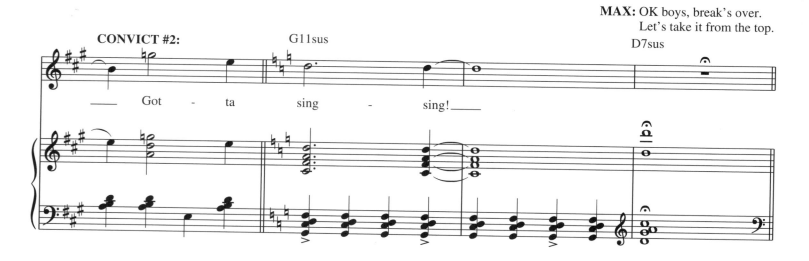

133

GOODBYE!

Music and Lyrics by
Mel Brooks

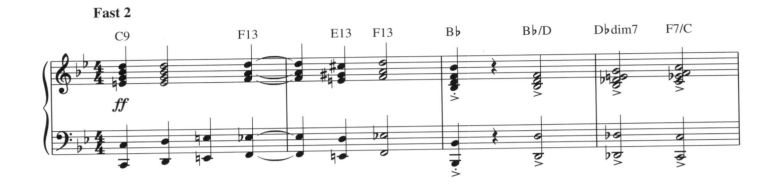

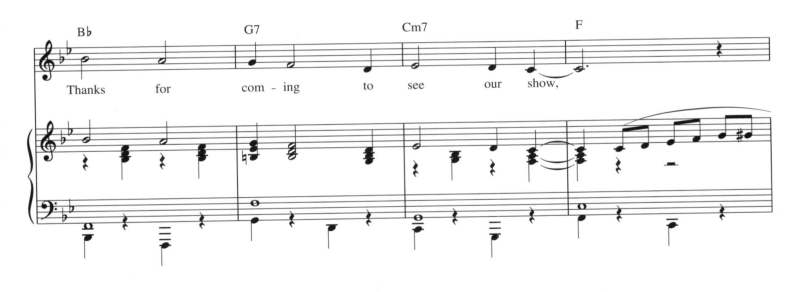

Thanks for com - ing to see our show,

sad to tell you we got to go. _____

THE ULTIMATE BROADWAY FAKE BOOK
4TH EDITION

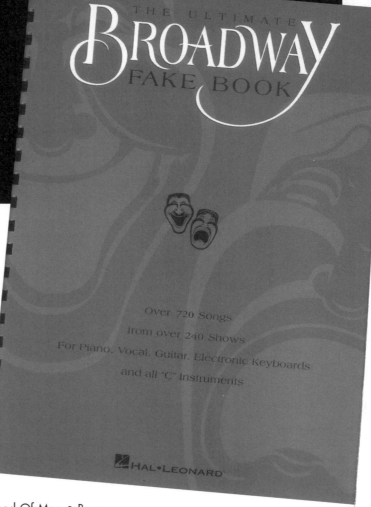

Over 600 pages offering 725 songs from more than 200 Broadway shows! Recently revised to include hits from *Jekyll & Hyde, Martin Guerre, Rent, Sunset Boulevard, Victor/Victoria*, and more! This is the definitive collection of Broadway music, featuring: • Song title index • Show title index • Composer & lyricist index • Synopses of each show.

SONGS INCLUDE:

After You've Gone • Ain't Misbehavin' • All I Ask Of You • All Of You • All The Things You Are • Angel Of Music • Another Op'nin' Another Show • Another Suitcase In Another Hall • Any Dream Will Do • As If We Never Said Goodbye • As Long As He Needs Me • At The Ballet • Bali Ha'i • The Ballad Of Sweeney Todd • Beauty And The Beast • Beauty School Dropout • Bess, You Is My Woman • Bewitched • Blue Skies • Bring Him Home • Brotherhood Of Man • Buenos Aires • Cabaret • Camelot • Can't Help Lovin' Dat Man • Caravan • Castle On A Cloud • Comedy Tonight • Consider Yourself • Dance: Ten Looks: Three • Day By Day • Do I Hear A Waltz? • Do-Re-Mi • Do You Hear The People Sing? • Don't Cry For Me Argentina • Down In The Depths (On The Ninetieth Floor) • Easter Parade • Edelweiss • Everything's Coming Up Roses • Ev'ry Time We Say Goodbye • Getting To Know You • Give My Regards To Broadway • Guys And Dolls • Have You Met Miss Jones? • Heat Wave • Hello, Dolly! • Hey, Look Me Over • How Are Things In Glocca Morra • How High The Moon • I Can Dream, Can't I? • I Could Have Danced All Night • I Don't Know How To Love Him • I Dreamed A Dream • I Remember It Well • I Won't Grow Up • I've Grown Accustomed To Her Face • If Ever I Would Leave You • If I Can't Love Her • If I Were A Man • If I Were A Rich Man • (I'm A) Yankee Doodle Dandy • The Impossible Dream • It's The Hard-Knock Life • June Is Bustin' Out All Over • Kids! • La Cage Aux Folles • The Lady Is A Tramp • Lambeth Walk • Last Night Of The World • Let Me Entertain You • A Little Night Music • Living In The Shadows • Lost In The Stars • Love Changes Everything • Luck Be A Lady • Make Someone Happy • Makin' Whoopee! • Mame • Maria • Me And My Girl • Memory • Mood Indigo • The Music Of The Night • My Funny Valentine • My Heart Belongs To Daddy • A New Life • Oh, What A Beautiful Mornin' • Oklahoma • Ol' Man River • On A Clear Day (You Can See Forever) • On My Own • On Your Toes • One • One Night In Bangkok • Only You • Paris By Night • The Party's Over • People • People Will Say We're In Love • Phantom of the Opera • Quiet Night • The Rain In Spain • Satin Doll • Send In The Clowns • Seventy-Six Trombones • Shall We Dance? • Smoke Gets In Your Eyes • So In Love • Some Enchanted Evening • Someone • Someone Like You • The Sound Of Music • Standing On The Corner • Starlight Express • Summer Nights • Sun and Moon • Sunrise, Sunset • The Surrey With The Fringe On Top • Tell Me On A Sunday • Tell Me To Go • Thank Heaven For Little Girls • There's No Business Like Show Business • This Is The Moment • Tomorrow • Too Darn Hot • Tradition • Try To Remember • Unexpected Song • Waitin' For The Light To Shine • What I Did For Love • Wishing You Were Somehow Here Again • With One Look • You'll Never Walk Alone • and more!

00240046 . . . . **$39.95**

Price, contents, and availability subject to change without notice.